Speaking and Liste
Book

McDougal Littell

GRADE SEVEN

McDougal Littell
A HOUGHTON MIFFLIN COMPANY
Evanston, Illinois Boston Dallas

ISBN 0-618-15372–1

4 5 6 7 8 9 – VEI – 04 03

Contents

Lesson

Name ______________________________ Date ______________

1 Asking Questions to Elicit Information

After listening to a speaker's presentation, you might have questions about the subject matter. A good and well-informed speaker will willingly address your concerns. After all, he or she will want to make sure that you—as an audience member—leave the presentation understanding the topic, not confused or unclear.

Use the questions below as guidelines for helping you form probing questions. Adapt these questions to make them more specific to the subject of the presentation.

The Topic or Thesis

- How and why did you choose this specific topic?
- Why is this topic specifically important or relevant?
- Am I correct in understanding that your thesis is ...?
- What is the main idea of this presentation?

The Supporting Evidence

- How did you collect evidence for your thesis?
- What additional evidence can you provide to support your claims?
- What evidence would opponents of your thesis use to challenge your thesis?
- How would you respond to or disprove their evidence?

Clarification

- Can you compare and contrast the following ideas ...?
- Can you explain in more detail who / what / when / where / why. . .?
- Can you provide a simpler or clearer example of ...?
- Can you restate or summarize your thesis/conclusion?

Follow-up

- How can I learn more about this specific aspect of the subject...?
- Where can I go to do more in-depth research on the subject?
- What are some other popular theories on this subject?
- What are some other related issues to this subject?
- How do you think this topic will change or evolve in the future?

Name ______________________ Date ______________

2 Determining Speaker's Attitude Toward the Subject

Many presentations are objective or impartial, but others are subjective and biased. Try to determine what a speaker's attitude is toward the subject. You can do this by paying careful attention to the type of presentation, the balance of content, the tone of the speaker, the range of evidence, and the validity of conclusions.

The next time you listen to a presentation, use the questions below to determine a speaker's attitude toward the subject.

Type of Presentation

- Is it an entertaining narrative?
- Is it an informative research presentation?
- Is it an interpretive oral summary?
- Is it a persuasive argument?

Balance of Content

- Are all sides of an argument or topic presented?
- Does the speaker spend more time on one side more than another?
- Does the speaker present each side fairly?

Tone of Speaker

- Does the speaker seem to favor one side of an argument over another?
- Does the speaker use loaded language or rhetorical devices?
- What emotions does the speaker display when addressing the subject? (excitement? anger? distrust?)

Range of Evidence

- Does the speaker present solid, relevant evidence for all sides of an argument?
- Does the speaker present more evidence for one side over another?
- Does the speaker dismiss or show disdain for any of the evidence?

Validity of Conclusions

- Are the speaker's conclusions well-supported by evidence and experts?
- Are the conclusions based more on facts or on opinions?
- Do the conclusions contradict widely-accepted knowledge?

Name ______________________________ Date ______________

3 Responding to Persuasion

A speaker may allow time at the end of a presentation for audience members to respond. If so, take advantage of this opportunity, especially if the presentation is a persuasive one. After all, you don't want to accept everything without thinking carefully about it. Instead, be willing to question, challenge, or affirm what was said. This willingness allows you to enhance your comprehension as well as to display intellectual curiosity, showing the speaker, your teacher, and other audience members that the topic is interesting enough for you to care about it.

Below are some ways that you can respond to a presentation.

Question

- I still don't understand why …
- I am unclear as to how …
- Am I to understand that …
- Is it your opinion that …
- Am I correct in assuming that …
- Can you clarify why …

Challenge

- But how does this relate to …
- And how would you respond to …
- What if this were to happen …
- How would argue against …
- What do you have to say about…
- There are others that say ...
- But aren't you contradicting …

Affirm

- I agree that …
- It makes sense to me that …
- I see where you're coming from when …
- I understand when you say …
- You're right on target with …

Activity: The next time you listen to a classmate's presentation, find three ways to question, challenge, or affirm what was said.

Name ______________________________ Date ______________

4 Matching Your Message with Purpose and Audience

Before you begin to prepare a speech, you first need to know *why* you are making the presentation and to *whom* you are presenting it. Understanding your purpose and audience will help you select an appropriate focus and organizational structure.

Use the checklist of questions below to help you match your message with its purpose and audience:

TO WHOM are you presenting?

- ☐ Fellow classmates
- ☐ An entire school assembly
- ☐ A group of teachers
- ☐ A panel of judges at a science fair
- ☐ A sports team during a timeout huddle
- ☐ Other

Tip: Keep your audience's point of view in mind as you write your speech.

WHAT is your reason for presenting?

- ☐ To share information
- ☐ To persuade listeners to do something
- ☐ To convince listeners of your views on a subject
- ☐ To entertain with a funny story
- ☐ Other

Tip: Your purpose directly affects your tone. Decide whether your purpose is best accomplished by being serious or humorous, casual or formal.

WHY does your speech matter?

- ☐ Because you performed in-depth research
- ☐ Because you have specialized knowledge in an area
- ☐ Because you have first-hand experience in the subject
- ☐ Because action is urgently required
- ☐ Other

Tip: Convince your audience that what you have to say matters.

HOW can you engage the members of your audience?

- ☐ By tailoring your information to the background and interests of the audience
- ☐ By presenting information logically
- ☐ My demonstrating your knowledge confidently
- ☐ By showing enthusiasm for what you are saying
- ☐ By using effective visual aids
- ☐ Other

Tip: Remember, it's not just what you present but how you present it.

Name ______________________________ Date ______________

5 Knowing Your Audience

Do you know how to prepare a speech so that it suits an audience? Are you aware that how you speak to a group of friends at lunch is drastically different from how you present a science project in class?

Activity: Check how well you know your audience by filling in your possible approach for each situation below. Take into account the language, tone, and gestures you would use. The first row is done for you. Discuss your answers with a classmate.

Audience: Group of classmates
Subject: Your latest book report
Possible Approach: *Use formal but captivating language. Keep tone serious. Use dramatic, lively gestures.*

Audience: Soccer teammates during a last game timeout
Subject: Your advice on how to make the game-winning shot
Possible Approach:

Audience: School assembly
Subject: Debating your opponent for class president
Possible Approach:

Audience: Group of friends on a camping trip
Subject: Telling a scary ghost story around the campfire
Possible Approach:

Audience: Your mother or father
Subject: Convincing them why they should extend your curfew
Possible Approach:

Audience: Members at a club meeting you are attending for the first time
Subject: Introducing yourself, explaining why you joined
Possible Approach:

Audience: Your best friend
Subject: Sharing the latest funny joke you heard
Possible Approach:

Name ______________________________ Date ______________

6 Writing Your Speech

Once you understand your purpose and audience, you are ready to get down to the basics of writing that speech. A good speech consists of several important elements, mentioned in the checklist below.

UNITY

- ☐ Did you organize the speech into single-idea paragraphs?
- ☐ Does each paragraph support the main idea of the speech?
- ☐ Did you use relevant and effective transitions between paragraphs?

LANGUAGE

- ☐ Did you select your language to match your audience and purpose?
- ☐ Did you choose words appropriately and effectively?
- ☐ Is your language clear, concise, and easy to follow?

EVIDENCE

- ☐ Did you state a clear position or perspective?
- ☐ Did you support your central idea with relevant facts, statistics, and other examples?
- ☐ Did you elaborate with specific details and examples?
- ☐ Did you use effective visual aids to present your evidence?
- ☐ Did you anticipate and address concerns and counterarguments?

EMPHASIS

- ☐ Did you assist your audience in following your main ideas by drawing attention to your most important points?
- ☐ Did you use your voice effectively, varying your rate, volume, pitch, and tone?
- ☐ Did you vary your facial expressions, hand gestures, and posture?
- ☐ Did you establish eye contact?

INTEREST

- ☐ Did you engage your audience with a compelling introduction?
- ☐ Did you end with a powerful or memorable conclusion?
- ☐ Did you use visual aids to hold your audience's attention?

Name ______________________________ Date ______________

7 Arranging Details Effectively and Persuasively

In a good presentation, your main thesis statement should be supported by clearly stated evidence. This evidence can be presented as details, reasons, descriptions, or examples. You should not, however, scatter evidence throughout your presentation in an unorganized way. Learn how to arrange the details of a speech effectively and persuasively, using the guidelines below.

Introduction

- If you're going to offer evidence in the introduction, remember that "less is more." Don't overload the audience.
- Focus on one strong example or statistic.
- Make sure your evidence is vivid, intense, or even startling, so that it grabs your audience's attention.
- Consider offering a piece of evidence that you can elaborate on thematically throughout the rest of the presentation. Your examples might all be taken from the world of sports, or animals, or astronomy.

Main Body

- Don't pick evidence randomly; pick *relevant* evidence.
- Try to provide at least one piece of supporting evidence for every new idea you introduce.
- Define concepts and terminology clearly.
- Offer simple, easy-to-understand examples for particularly complex ideas.
- When possible, include well-labeled diagrams or illustrations. These might be useful for visual design ideas or for reporting on experiments.

Conclusion

- Remember that the conclusion is not the place to add a flurry of statistics. Your audience needs time to absorb such details.
- As in the introduction, leave your audience with one strong or compelling piece of evidence.
- Offer something memorable that will leave your audience thinking about your presentation long after it is over.

In General

- Assume your audience knows *nothing* about the subject of your presentation.
- Realize that your choice of evidence directly relates to how well your audience will understand a complex concept.
- Use familiar examples that your audience can relate to and will understand.
- Choose evidence that is exciting and entertaining, rather than dull or bland.

Name ______________________________ Date ______________

8 Choosing Presentation Aids

Think of your oral presentation as an opportunity not just to talk about your ideas, but also to *demonstrate* them. This is where visual aids and media displays come into play, and there is a wide variety at your disposal. In deciding to add visual aids to your oral presentation, consider your audience, the purpose of your speech, and the best way to get your message across.

Decide which visual aids are most appropriate to the organization, structure, and presentation of your information. Use the chart below to help you in making your selection.

Type	Advantages	Special Considerations
Slides	Show real people, places, and things	Require special projection equipment
Maps	Show specific locations and relations of events	Need to be large, simple, and well-labeled
Charts and Graphs	Present facts and statistics visually	Need to be accurate and well-labeled
Drawings	Illustrate real or imaginary ideas or things	Need to be large, simple, and well-labeled
Photos	Show real people, places, and things	Need to be passed around the room
CDs	Provide sound effects and music that help create an atmosphere or illustrate a point	Require special sound equipment
Web Sites	Provide multimedia sources of information on your topic	May need to be projected on a screen for proper viewing

Name ______________________________ Date ______________

9 Supporting Opinions with Evidence and Visuals

Adding appropriate visual aids and media displays to your oral presentation can help enliven and elaborate on your content. Be sure to use visuals to support and supplement your main ideas, not to serve as fancy distractions for your audience. Remember to include an interesting variety, and know how to handle each of them skillfully.

Use the checklist below as you prepare to add visual aids and media displays to your speech.

Choice

- Consider your audience and purpose.
- Decide which aids best reflect your information (*Examples:* charts and graphics for presenting statistics; slides and diagrams for presenting images).
- Choose a few relevant aids.
- Choose aids that are convenient and easy to use.

Variety

- Evaluate the available presentation aids.
- Consider what types of visuals will best capture your audience's interest.
- Keep your materials varied, but also relevant.

Design

- Use visuals that are simple and well-labeled.
- Use bright, vibrant colors.
- Make sure visuals are large enough to be seen by everyone in the audience.

Use

- Mark your note cards to remind you where and when to use your aids.
- Learn how to operate any necessary equipment, such as projectors, computers, and so on.
- Make sure that all necessary equipment is available and working properly.
- Rehearse your speech *with* presentation aids several times.

Activity: Watch a documentary on television. Keep track of visuals used to present information. How did they support the verbal part? Were the aids simple, varied, and well-designed?

Name ____________________ Date ____________

10 Sustaining Audience Interest and Attention

Audiences hate having to sit through boring and lifeless speeches, but you don't have to fall into this trap. The next time you make a presentation, keep the members of your audience interested and on the edge of their seats by knowing and using the following strategies.

Start strong, finish strong

- Use a "hook" or idea that will engage your audience from the beginning.
- Pose an interesting question or statement to capture listeners' attention.
- Conclude with a powerful example or anecdote to reinforce your message.
- Leave your audience with a memorable last line.

Vary your voice

- Control and vary volume to emphasize and persuade.
- Vary pitch for interest, and "build" to a strong conclusion.
- If narrating a story, use a range of voices to bring unforgettable characters to life.
- Establish a compelling rhythm or pace.

Express with body language

- Use animated facial expressions to illustrate emotion.
- Use direct eye contact to connect with audience.
- Use forceful hand gestures to emphasize or illustrate information.
- Use good posture to express confidence and enthusiasm.

Employ powerful language

- Use a variety of dynamic verbs and adjectives.
- Choose one perfect word rather than three average ones.
- Create a specific setting for your audience to experience.
- Appeal to your audience's five senses.

Offer Strong Evidence

- Present facts and statistics that are exciting, humorous, or even shocking.
- Use modern, current examples that an audience can relate to.
- Use evidence in the form of a story or an anecdote.
- Enhance your speech with captivating, relevant visuals; sound effects; and props.

Engage Your Audience

- Encourage your audience to participate.
- Ask audience members if they have any questions or comments.
- Pose your own rhetorical questions.
- Use presentation aids and props that they can touch or hold.

Name ______________________ Date ______________

11 Nonverbal Strategies

Effective public speaking requires a strong physical presence and a clear voice. The following nonverbal strategies will help you to speak more effectively and to present information to an audience with conviction and authority.

Be aware of your posture. Good *posture,* or how straight you stand, conveys confidence. Before speaking to an audience, check your posture in a mirror. Make sure your shoulders do not slump and that your feet are firmly planted. Good posture also allows you to breathe better, which is essential for clear and comfortable speaking.

Adjust your body language. Like posture, *body language,* or how you nonverbally communicate with other people, can be controlled. Before making a presentation in public:

- Practice before a mirror
- Make sure you stand comfortably with your hands at your sides or in front of you
- Avoid folding your arms
- Avoid sudden or jerky movements and odd facial expressions that can draw attention away from what you are saying

Keeping your audience's needs in mind, rather than your own worries, will help you avoid self-conscious mannerisms.

Handle visual aids smoothly. It is important to handle note cards, reading material, and other visual aids in a graceful way that does not distract from speaking. Before you make your presentation:

- Arrange visual aids on the desk or lectern in the order in which you will be using them
- Number note cards or pages so that you can keep them in order
- Hold note cards close enough to see, but not so close that they block your face or muffle your voice

Be aware of differences when speaking with a group. Sometimes several speakers or actors give a presentation together. It is important that the group of speakers interacts well instead of interrupting each other. Try to prearrange a signal or word that indicates when one speaker is finished so that the next speaker may begin.

Name ______________________________ Date ______________

12 Listening Actively

When you have something important to say, you want to make sure that people are listening. But are *you* a good listener? Remember that hearing is not the same as listening. When you hear, you use your ear to take in sounds and words. When you *listen*, you also use your eyes to focus on the speaker and your mind to process what is being said.

Activity: The next time you listen to a teacher's lecture, a classmate's presentation, or an information program on television, use the chart below to evaluate your active listening skills.

	Did I . . .
Before Listening	• Keep an open mind and not prejudge the speaker before he or she spoke? • Prepare myself by reviewing what I already know about the subject? • Listen with a purpose?
While Listening	• Block out distractions and stay focused? • Look for signals of the main ideas? • Take notes, if appropriate? • Look for relationships between ideas? • Identify tone, mood, and use of gestures?
After Listening	• Review notes taken? • Ask questions, when possible, for clarification? • Summarize, paraphrase, and evaluate?

Name ________________________________ Date ______________

13 GUIDELINES: How to Recognize Main Ideas

- Did you listen for ideas presented first or last? List them here.

- Did you listen for ideas repeated several times for emphasis? List them here.

- Did you note statements that begin with phrases such as "My point is..." or "The important thing to remember is..."? List them here.

- Did you pay attention to ideas presented in a loud voice or with forceful gestures? List them here.

- Did you think about what the speaker was trying to tell you? Summarize the message here.

- In a multimedia presentation, did you note points the speaker had reproduced on a chart or on any other visual aid? List them here.

Name ______________________________ Date ______________

14 GUIDELINES: How to Evaluate What You Hear

- What is the purpose of the talk and does the speaker achieve it? State the purpose here.

- Does the information make sense? Does it contradict anything you already know?

- Are ideas presented in an interesting and logical way?

- Are points supported with facts and details? List them here.

- Do you still have any questions after hearing the talk? List them here.

- Do you agree with what the speaker said? Why or why not? Write your reasons here.

Name ______________________ Date ____________

15 GUIDELINES: How to Listen Critically

- Are you aware of the speaker's purpose in addressing you? State the purpose here.

- Does the speaker seem confident in his or her knowledge of the subject?

- Does the speaker convince with concrete evidence rather than creative rhetoric? List evidence here.

- Are you able to distinguish between personal opinions and verifiable facts? List the opinions and the facts here.

- Does the speaker use faulty or misleading persuasive devices? List them here.

- Did you clarify any information that seemed unclear or confusing?

Name ______________________________ Date ____________

16 Providing Feedback on Coherence and Logic

A *coherent* and *logical* speech is one that is clear, connected, and sensible. It flows well and builds towards a reasonable conclusion. Its individual parts work together as a whole. In a perfect world, all speeches you listen to would be coherent and logical. But if and when they are not, providing specific, constructive feedback to the speaker is your way of helping a speaker learn and improve.

Use the guidelines below to help you analyze and provide feedback on the coherence and logic of a speech.

Thesis	**My Comments/Feedback**
• Is it directly related to the subject of the presentation? • Is it stated in a clear, concise, and to-the-point way? • Does it contradict anything you already know? • Is it a fresh, new idea or simply a rehash of old ideas?	
Supporting Details	**My Comments/Feedback**
• Does the speaker use relevant, easy-to-understand examples and details? • Do the examples directly relate to both the subject and the thesis? • Do the examples work together as a group, or are they random and disconnected? • Did the speaker use a variety of authoritative sources?	

Name ______________________________ Date ______________

16 Providing Feedback on Coherence and Logic *continued*

Conclusion	My Comments/Feedback
• Does the conclusion follow logically, based on the thesis and supporting details? • Is the conclusion backed by fact, reason, and analysis, or does it seem more like an unsupported opinion? • Are you persuaded by the conclusion, or do you at least feel that it was presented rationally?	

Strengths/Weaknesses	My Comments/Feedback
• What was the strongest part of the speech? What was the weakest? • How could the speaker improve the preparation or selection of material? • What one or two changes would make the speaker's message clearer?	

Name ______________________________ Date ______________

17 Providing Feedback on Delivery and Impact

No matter how many facts, statistics, and examples a speaker provides you with during a presentation, in the end you are left with an overall impression of how that speech affected—or left an impact—on you, both intellectually and emotionally. Content and delivery play equal roles in determining how well you receive a presentation. Both have to be strong in order for you to come away feeling fulfilled, rather than disappointed.

Use the guidelines below to help you analyze and provide feedback on the delivery and impact of a speech.

Content	My Comments/ Feedback
• Does the information make sense?	
• Are points supported with facts, details, and logic?	
• What is the purpose of the talk and does the speaker achieve it?	
• Is the speaker convincing? Why or why not?	
• Do you still have questions after hearing the talk?	

Delivery	My Comments/ Feedback
• Did the speaker speak clearly and understandably?	
• Did the speaker seem excited or inspired by what he or she was saying?	
• Did the speaker maintain eye contact and use effective gestures? Did the speaker's body language or movements interfere with the content in any way?	
• What aspects of the delivery were strongest? Which were weakest? (Consider enunciation, pitch, pace, volume, emphasis, and projection.)	

Name ______________________________ Date ______________

17 Providing Feedback on Delivery and Impact *continued*

Impact	My Comments/ Feedback
• How interested were you by the subject of the presentation?	
• Did your interest increase, decrease, or stay the same as the speech progressed?	
• How interesting and/or effective were the examples and visual aids used?	
• What emotions, if any, did you feel during the speech? Did you feel anger? inspiration? confusion?	
• What was your overriding emotion at the end of the speech? Were you excited? bored? indifferent?	
• How does whatever you were feeling affect your overall impression of the speech?	

Name ______________________________ Date ______________

18 Analyzing Effects on the Viewer

In a world that uses television to bombard you with "information" on a daily basis, it is important that you learn to become an aware and discriminating viewer of both news and video or film. What distinguishes a good news report from a bad one? What makes a film adaptation of a novel or short story effective? Is a program better because of its reliable sources or its fancy graphics?

A thorough news report will usually provide details that answer the questions *who*, *what*, *when*, *where*, and *why* (and sometimes *how*). Additionally, facts, pictures or descriptions, quotations, and other details give you a fuller understanding of what's being communicated.

Activity: The next time you watch a news report on television or a video, use the evaluation form below to judge the effectiveness of the report or the story and its impact on you, the viewer.

Subject ______________________________

____

Criteria	Poor	Fair	Good
Effectively explains who, what, when, where, and why			
Uses facts, not opinions (news only)			
Avoids bias, sensationalism, or misleading persuasive devices (news only)			
Presents a balanced report of all sides of a story (news only)			
Uses relevant pictures, voiceovers, descriptions, or images, characters, and dialogue for clarification of what's happening in the story			
Uses quotations from relevant authorities, experts, or texts			
Presents the story in a way that's easy to understand			

Overall Impact: ______________________________

Name ______________________________ Date ______________

19 Identifying Techniques Used to Achieve Effects

Electronic journalism uses a combination of images, text, and sounds to create a "package" of information for its viewers. Content is important, but so are the techniques used to capture your attention as a viewer. News programs have to do more than spew out facts to keep you from flipping to another TV channel. They also have to be dynamic, interesting, and even entertaining. The same is true of movies—both film and video.

Activity: The next time you watch a program on television or video, pay specific attention to the various components that make up the story. Use the guidelines below to identify and evaluate the techniques used to keep you watching.

Images

- What pictures or video images accompany the piece?
- Are these images specifically relevant to the story?
- Visually, are these images interesting? exciting? shocking?
- Do the images make you want to continue watching the piece?
- If charts or graphs are used, are they clear and well-labeled? (news only)
- If people are being quoted, is it acceptable simply to hear their voiceovers or does it help to see them talking? Why or why not? (news only)

Text (news only)

- What is the title of the piece? Does it grab your attention? How?
- What textual graphics accompany the visuals?
- What kind of font and colors are used?
- Is the text used specifically related to the information?

Sounds

- What kind of music is used at the beginning of the story? (Is it lively? urgent? eerie?)
- How does the music inform you about what will follow?
- What background sound accompanies the visuals of the piece? (gun fire? police sirens? the laughter of a crowd?)
- Are the sound effects of the piece directly related to the information, or do they seem more like distraction or entertainment?
- In news stories, how does the anchor or the reporter use his or her voice to make the piece seem more interesting or important?

Overall Evaluation: ______________________________

Name ______________________________ Date ______________

20 Creating a Narrative Presentation

Use the chart below to help you create and develop your next narrative presentation.

Elements	Questions to Consider	My Ideas
Establish a Setting	What is the time, place, and circumstance in which the action takes place? Is the setting appropriate to the subject matter?	
Create a Plot	What happens in the story? Should the plot be funny? tragic? suspenseful? How do events unfold? over what period of time?	
Determine a Point of View	Who is the main character of the story? What is his or her point of view?	
Use Effective Language	What kind of sensory details will be most effective or appropriate for the story? How can I help the audience experience what's happening?	
Employ Narrative Devices	Which devices (dialogue, language, suspense, props, sound effects) can I use to keep the narrative interesting?	
Focus on the Delivery	How can I bring the narrative to life? How should I speak? stand? gesture?	

Name ______________________________ Date ______________

21 GUIDELINES: How to Analyze a Narrative Presentation

- Did you choose a setting that makes sense and contributes to a believable narrative?
- Does your plot help create the right mood for your audience?
- Is your character—and his or her point of view—realistic and memorable?
- Did you use strong, sensory language that allows your audience to experience the story?
- Did you use a range of narrative devices to keep your audience interested?
- Did you deliver effectively?

Evaluating a Narrative Presentation

Scoring: 1 = poor; 2–4 = fair; 5 = average; 6–8 = above average; 9–10 = excellent

Attribute	Score
How believable is the setting?	
How well is the mood created?	
How realistic is the main character?	
How memorable is the main character?	
How effective is the language in involving the audience?	
How effective are the narrative devices in involving the audience?	
How effective is the delivery?	

Name ______________________ Date ______________

22 Creating an Oral Summary

Use the chart below to help you create and develop your next oral summary.

Elements	Questions to Consider	My Ideas
Introducing Subject	What is the article or book about? Who is the author? Why did he or she write it? What is the main idea?	
Providing Supporting Details	What are the significant details of the piece? What evidence supports the main idea? What specific, relevant quotes can I use from the text?	
Using Your Own Words	How do I deliver the information simply and clearly, so that the audience can easily understand it? How would I paraphrase the story in my own words?	
Conveying Comprehension	How can I demonstrate an in-depth understanding of the piece? How do I move beyond superficial details? What questions might the audience ask? How would I answer them?	

Name ______________________________ Date ______________

23 GUIDELINES: How to Analyze an Oral Summary

- Did you introduce the subject clearly?
- Did you present the main idea(s) early in your presentation?
- Did you discuss the supporting details of the speech, using quotes when appropriate?
- Did you summarize the information using your own clear and simplified words?
- Did you show your audience that you really understand the piece?

Evaluating an Oral Summary

Scoring: 1 = poor; 2–4 = fair; 5 = average; 6–8 = above average; 9–10 = excellent

Attribute	Score
How well has the subject been introduced?	
How clearly were the main ideas presented?	
How effective are the examples and supporting details?	
How appropriate are the quotes?	
How easy is it to understand the information presented?	
How well did the speaker communicate understanding of the piece?	

Name ______________________________ Date ______________

24 Creating a Research Presentation

Use the chart below to help you create and develop your next research presentation.

Elements	Questions to Consider	My Ideas
Targeting Audience	What might the audience already know about the subject? What might they still want to know? Keeping this in mind, how can I develop a focused, organized presentation?	
Introducing Topic	What kind of interesting question or fascinating fact can I use to grab the audience's attention?	
Conveying Clear and Accurate Perspective	How do I explain to the audience the purpose of my presentation? What do I hope they will get out of it? How did I go about collecting the information to present?	
Presenting Research	What is the "meat" of my presentation? What evidence, statistics, and details did I gain from the research? What sources should I cite? What effective visual aids can I use?	

Name ______________________ Date ______________

25 GUIDELINES: How to Analyze a Research Presentation

- Did you think about your audience's previous knowledge of the subject?
- Did you hook your audience with an interesting question or fact?
- Did you explain the purpose and framework of the presentation?
- Did you explain the process you used to collect information?
- Did you present your research clearly and concisely?
- Did you cite a variety of sources and use effective presentation aids?

Evaluating a Research Presentation

Scoring: 1 = poor; 2–4 = fair; 5 = average; 6–8 = above average; 9–10 = excellent

Attribute	Score
How well has the audience's previous knowledge been taken into account?	
How interesting was the introduction?	
How clearly was the purpose of the presentation conveyed?	
How clearly is the research presented?	
How effective are the visual aids?	

Name ______________________________ Date ______________

26 Creating a Persuasive Presentation

Use the chart below to help you create and develop your next persuasive presentation.

Elements	Questions to Consider	My Ideas
Research	What do I already know about the subject? What do I still need to know? Am I aware of all points-of-view on the topic? Do I understand their "pros" as well as "cons"?	
Point of View	After analyzing all the information, what is my personal position on the subject? What is the best way to present it to my audience?	
Position	What supporting evidence can I use to back up my position? Where can I find relevant facts, statistics, and experts' quotes?	
Defense	What questions or doubts might the audience have about my position? How can I counteract them persuasively, before they are even raised?	
Delivery	How can I engage the audience? What is the best way to persuade them? How do I show them I really believe in what I am saying?	

Name ______________________________ Date ______________

27 GUIDELINES: How to Analyze a Persuasive Presentation

- Did you present a clear statement or argument?
- Did you support your argument with convincing facts?
- Did you use sound logic in developing the argument?
- Did you use voice, facial expression, gestures, and posture effectively?
- Did you hold the audience's interest?

Evaluating a Persuasive Presentation

Scoring: 1 = poor; 2–4 = fair; 5 = average; 6–8 = above average; 9–10 = excellent

Attribute	Score
How well does the speaker present his or her argument?	
How convincing are the supporting facts?	
How logical is the argument?	
How effective is the use of voice, facial expressions, gestures, and posture?	
How interested is the audience in the presentation?	

Name ______________________ Date ____________

28 Working in a Group

Assigning roles when working in a group is a great way to keep the discussion focused and on track. Individuals who know and understand their specific tasks will ultimately be more productive members of a group as a whole.

The chart below highlights some of the roles you can assign in your next group discussion:

Role	Responsibilities	Selection Process
Chairperson	• Introduces topic for discussion • Explains the goal or purpose of the meeting • Participates in the discussion • Keeps discussion focused • Helps resolve conflict and maintain fairness	Choose someone who is fair, confident, well-organized, and authoritative.
Recorder	• Takes notes on discussion • Participates in discussion • Organizes and writes up notes • Distributes notes or "minutes" to entire group	Choose someone who is alert, attentive, well-organized, and has legible handwriting.
Participants	• Contribute facts or ideas to discussion • Respond constructively to others' ideas • Reach agreement or vote on final decision	Choose people who know the subject well, are opinionated but tactful, have strong speaking and listening skills, and are good at brainstorming.

Name ______________________________ Date ______________

29 GUIDELINES: How to Analyze a Group Discussion

- Did you take turns speaking?
- Did you listen attentively to each speaker and take notes?
- Did you ask questions or comment on others' ideas?
- Did you speak clearly and confidently?
- Did you avoid interrupting someone who was speaking?
- Did you avoid using disrespectful language?
- Did you avoid dismissing others' ideas without evaluating them?

Evaluating a Group Discussion

Scoring: 1 = poor; 2–4 = fair; 5 = average; 6–8 = above average; 9–10 = excellent

Attribute	Score
How much does everyone get a chance to participate?	
How attentively is each person listened to?	
How often do the group members ask questions or make comments?	
How clearly do the group members speak?	
How well do the group members keep from interrupting?	
How respectful are group members to each other?	
How thoughtful are responses to other members of the group?	

Name ______________________ Date ____________

30 Conducting Interviews

Use the chart below to help you arrange and conduct your next interview.

Elements	Questions to Consider	My Ideas
Before the Interview	What do I want to learn? Who can give me the information I need? What do I need to learn about my subject before the interview? Which are my most important questions? How can I phrase the questions to get the most information?	
During the Interview	Do I want to bring along someone to take notes? How much time will I allow for the answers to each question? What will I do if I disagree with the person I am interviewing? What will I do if the interviewee goes off on a tangent?	
After the Interview	What are the most important ideas that I want to remember? What statements do I want to use as direct quotations? When can I follow up?	

Name ______________________________ Date ______________

31 GUIDELINES: How to Analyze an Interview

- Did you identify an appropriate person to interview?
- Did you research sufficient background information?
- Did you prepare open-ended, challenging questions?
- Did you ask questions clearly and listen carefully?
- Did you follow up on interesting responses?
- Did you avoid arguing with the interviewee?
- Did you take notes?
- Did you send a thank-you note?

Evaluating an Interview

Scoring: 1 = poor; 2–4 = fair; 5 = average; 6–8 = above average; 9–10 = excellent

Attribute	Score
How good a subject is the interviewee?	
How complete is the background research?	
How interesting are the questions?	
How accurate are the quotes?